ORB WEAVERS

Blaine Wiseman

SPIDERS

www.av2books.com

Step 1
Go to **www.av2books.com**

Step 2
Enter this unique code

BMQUYISP1

Step 3
Explore your interactive eBook!

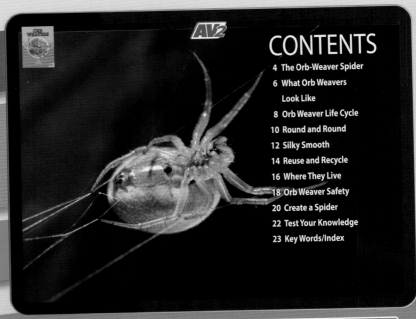

CONTENTS

AV2 is optimized for use on any device

Your interactive eBook comes with...

Contents
Browse a live contents page to easily navigate through resources

Audio
Listen to sections of the book read aloud

Videos
Watch informative video clips

Weblinks
Gain additional information for research

Try This!
Complete activities and hands-on experiments

Key Words
Study vocabulary, and complete a matching word activity

Quizzes
Test your knowledge

Slideshows
View images and captions

... and much, much more!

SPIDERS

ORB WEAVERS

Contents

Introduction

The Orb–Weaver Spider

When people think of a spider, they often imagine it dangling in the middle of a round web that looks like a wheel, or an **orb**. This is an orb-weaver spider.

Orb weavers are some of the most common spiders. They are found in almost every part of the world.

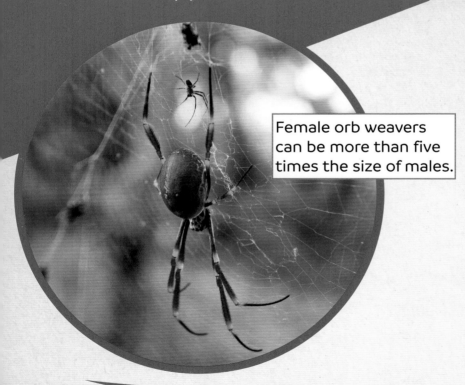

Female orb weavers can be more than five times the size of males.

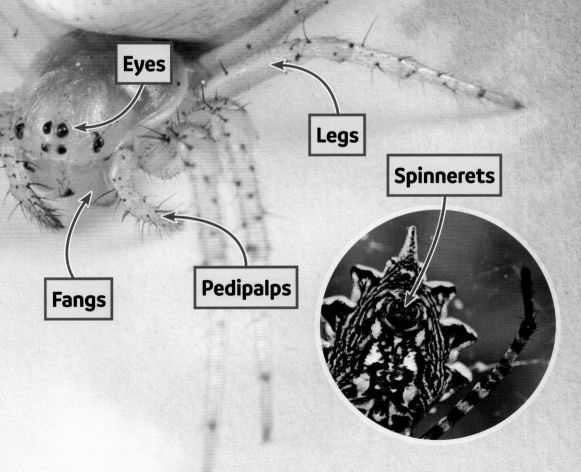

Eyes

Legs

Spinnerets

Fangs

Pedipalps

What Orb Weavers Look Like

There are thousands of different **species** of orb weaver. They can have many different looks. Orb weavers can be large or small. Some are colorful, while others are plain.

All orb weavers have spinnerets. They are used to make silk. Orb weavers have eight long legs. Their eight tiny eyes are in two rows of four. Orb-weaver spiders do not see very well. They use **vibrations** to feel when dangers or **prey** are near.

There are more than **3,000 types** of orb-weaver spiders.

Most spiders have two claws at the end of each leg. Orb weavers **have three**.

Orb Weaver Life Cycle

Orb-weaver spiders only live for about one year. Females lay several hundred eggs in the fall. They hatch in the spring.

Spiderlings leave the nest as soon as they hatch. They are so small that they can ride the wind to a new home. The spiderlings use silk to catch the wind like a sail. This is called ballooning.

When male orb weavers grow up, they look for a **mate**. Male spiders do not live as long as females. Sometimes, the female will eat her mate.

Sizing It Up

Zebra Jumping Spider
Leg Span: 0.3 inches
(0.8 centimeters)

**Western Black
Widow Spider**
Leg Span: 1.5 inches (3.8 cm)

Carolina Wolf Spider
Leg Span: 3 inches (7.6 cm)

**Giant Golden
Orb Weaver**
Leg Span: 5.9 inches (15 cm)

**Giant Huntsman
Spider**
Leg Span: 12 inches
(30.5 cm)

Goliath Birdeater
Leg Span: 12 inches
(30.5 cm)

Orb Weavers

Round and Round

To make a web, an orb weaver dangles a piece of sticky silk. It waits until the wind carries the silk to a wall or branch. Then, the spider uses more silk to make a "Y" shape hanging from this line. Next, the spider adds more lines of silk, like **spokes** on a wheel, from the center of the "Y." This is called the frame of the web.

Next, the spider builds the orb part of the web. It walks in circles and attaches sticky silk to the frame. When the web is finished, the spider sits in the middle. It waits for prey to get stuck.

Spot the sticky silk circle!

Silky Smooth

Orb weavers make different types of silk for different needs. They use tough silk to build the frame of their web and wrap up their prey. They use sticky silk for the orb. Egg sacs are made of strong silk to protect the eggs.

Different types of silk come from different **glands** in the spider's body. Orb weavers can quickly switch between different types of silk when building their webs.

Reuse and Recycle

An orb weaver's web can get messy. This is why many orb-weaver spiders build a new web every day. First, the spider eats its old web. Eating the silk gives the spider energy to help it build a new web.

When a spider eats its old web, it also eats things that are attached to it. This can include water drops. Orb weavers can get all of the water they need from these drops.

In 2012, two artists finished making a cape using silk from more than **1 million** orb weavers.

Orb-weaver spider webs can be as large as **3 feet** (0.9 meters) across.

Map
Where They Live

Different species of orb weavers can be found all over the world. Many orb-weaver spiders live in areas close to humans. They make their webs in gardens, yards, basements, attics, and many other areas built by people.

Orb Weavers around the World

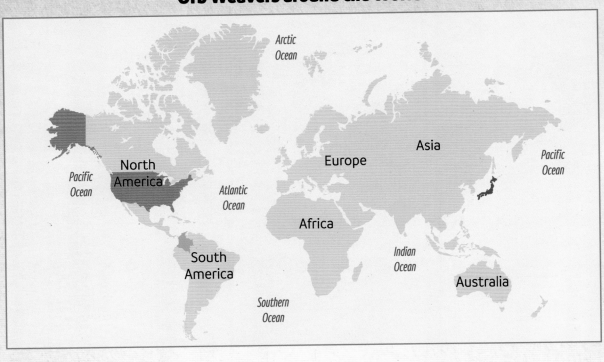

LEGEND

India	Japan	Land
Colombia	United States	Ocean

Scale 3,000 miles
0 3,000 kilometers

Giant Golden Orb Weaver

Japan

Giant golden orb weavers are the biggest orb-weaver spiders in the world. They are found in many countries, including Japan. Giant golden orb weavers can catch and eat prey as large as bats and birds.

Cross Spider

United States

Cross spiders came to the United States from Europe. They have white dots on their back that make the shape of a cross.

Bolas Spider

Colombia

Bolas spiders are orb weavers that do not build webs. Instead, they use a silk line with a sticky drop at the end to catch moths. One species from Colombia is named after Dizzy Dean, a famous baseball player.

Long-Horned Orb Weaver

India

The long-horned orb weaver is found in India and many other parts of Asia. It has long, curved spikes on its back that look like horns. People think the horns might scare away other animals.

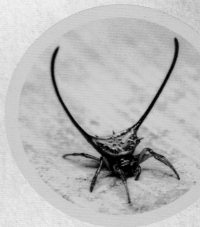

Orb Weaver Safety

Orb-weaver spiders are not dangerous to humans. If an orb weaver bites, it is because it felt threatened. A bite may cause some swelling which usually goes away after a few hours.

These spiders help people more than they hurt them. They hunt and eat **pests** such as flies and wasps. Some people use them to protect important **crops**. If people find an orb weaver in their home, they can safely move it outside using a jar or cup.

Create a Spider

There are many different kinds of spiders in the world. They all have certain features in common. However, each spider also has its own features. They help the spider live in its home.

Make your own spider by answering the following questions:

1. What is your spider called?
2. Where does it live?
3. What features does it share with other spiders?
4. What features help it live in its home? How do these features do this?
5. What does your spider look like?
6. Use pencils, markers, or crayons to draw your spider living in its home. Make sure to include all of its features.

Test Your Knowledge

1

How many claws do orb weavers have on each leg?

2

How do orb-weaver spiderlings travel through the air?

3

What shape is an orb weaver's web?

4

What is a spider web made of?

5

What do orb weavers do with their old webs?

6

Which orb-weaver spiders do not build webs?

7

Which orb weavers may eat birds?

8

Are orb-weaver spiders dangerous to humans?

ANSWERS 1. Three 2. By ballooning 3. Round 4. Silk 5. Eat them 6. Bolas spiders 7. Giant golden orb weavers 8. No

Key Words

crops: plants that are grown as food

glands: body parts that produce special materials or remove harmful materials from the body

mate: one member of a pair of animals that can reproduce, or have children

orb: a circular shape

pests: animals that harm or bother humans

prey: animals that are hunted by others

species: a group of closely related animals or plants

spiderlings: baby spiders

spokes: bars that join the center of a wheel with the outer rim

vibrations: when something is shaking or trembling

Index

Get the best of both worlds.

AV2 bridges the gap between print and digital.

The expandable resources toolbar enables quick access to content including **videos**, **audio**, **activities**, **weblinks**, **slideshows**, **quizzes**, and **key words**.

Animated videos make static images come alive.

Resource icons on each page help readers to further **explore key concepts**.

Published by AV2
14 Penn Plaza, 9th Floor New York, NY 10122
Website: www.av2books.com

Library of Congress Control Number: 2019957561

ISBN 978-1-7911-2312-3 (hardcover)
ISBN 978-1-7911-2313-0 (softcover)
ISBN 978-1-7911-2314-7 (multi-user eBook)
ISBN 978-1-7911-2315-4 (single-user eBook)

Printed in Guangzhou, China
1 2 3 4 5 6 7 8 9 0   24 23 22 21 20

052020
101119

Designer: Terry Paulhus Project Coordinator: John Willis

Every reasonable effort has been made to trace ownership and to obtain permission to reprint copyright material. The publisher would be pleased to have any errors or omissions brought to its attention so that they may be corrected in subsequent printings.

The publisher acknowledges Alamy, Getty Images, iStock, Minden Pictures, and Shutterstock as its primary image suppliers for this title.

View new titles and product videos at www.av2books.com